WHAT ARE WE NOT FOR

WHAT ARE WE NOT FOR

poems by

Tommye Blount

DURHAM, NORTH CAROLINA

WHAT ARE WE NOT FOR

Published in the United States of America

Library of Congress Cataloging-in-Publication Data

Blount, Tommye
What Are We Not For: poems / by Tommye Blount
p. cm.
ISBN-13: 978-1-4951-5763-9

Book design by Flying Hand Studio

Published by
BULL CITY PRESS
1217 Odyssey Drive
Durham, NC 27713

www.BullCityPress.com

ACKNOWLEDGMENTS

First, gratitude goes to the editors, readers, and staff of the following journals for giving space to these poems—sometimes in different form:

New England Review: "What Are We Not For" and
    "The Black Umbrella"
Four Way Review: "Bareback Aubade with the Dog,"
    "And the Dog Comes Back," "The Runts," and "Lycanthropy"
Poetry: "The Bug" and "The Tongue"
Transition Magazine: "The Bug Chaser"
Indiana Review: "Geppetto's Lament"
Phantom: "The Suit"
The Offing: "There Is Always a Face to Tend To"
Vinyl: "The House"
The Collagist: "& Bees"

"The Bug" was reprinted in *The Poetry Review*

There is no way this collection would exist without support, either directly or indirectly, from the following individuals and organizations:

A. Van Jordan, Adam Giannelli, Airea D. Matthews, Alison Meyers, All of you at Warren Wilson MFA Program for Writers, Aricka Foreman, Bread Loaf Writers' Conference, Bull City Press, C. Dale Young, Carl Phillips, Carrie Mar, Cave Canem, Cornelius Eady, David Blair, Debra Allbery, Eavan Boland, Ellen Bryant Voigt, Francine Conley, francine j. harris, Friends of Writers, Gabrielle Calvocoressi, Jamaal May, Joan Aleshire, Kahn Davison, Laura Swearingen-Steadwell, Lia Greenwell, Martha Rhodes, Matthew Olzmann, Nandi Comer, Nathan McClain, Rachel Brownson, Ross White, Scheherazade W. Parrish, Tarfia Faizullah, The Grind, The Holden Family, Tiya Kunaiyi-Harrell, Toi Derricotte, Vievee Francis, and WWWN.

A special thank you to LaShawn Hughes and LaRon Ward.

For Glory and James Blount—the constellations I move under.

CONTENTS

Bareback Aubade with the Dog

Thicker than its master's thigh,
I saw that dog gnawing its leash—
and didn't I know better? Knowing my fear

of dogs, I thought, "If I walk faster
and stay calm, then—"

That leash, thin as *Yes*, snapped. Of course
the dog snapped too and I
wasn't fast enough—only two legs then

instead of four. I was afraid, yes,
but I didn't run. With my eyes shut,

I braced for what comes to those afraid
of what they refuse to see. But
that time, the dog headed for the lake.

It passed me by and I watched
the water gulp it down—its paws and then

its legs and then its flanks and then gone
was the scruffy heart
of its head. Wasn't I sure it would not resurface

when it did? What sunlight there was
caught in its mouth a small body—its
slim head bucked twice more
against the water's vermillion ripple.

But the Weather, the Weather

"At least the sun's out," I tell the man I'm borrowing for an hour.
Of the last round of storms, I ramble off words like "rough,"
"harsh," "bad." I go on about last winter—this
day, about a year ago. Then, like that, I shut my mouth

around the rough ramble of wordlessness. *But there are always storms
drawn to the Panhandle,* I think as steel drums beg from the Key West ad
again. Bare-wristed and grinning, without a care for what day or year it is,
the man spins his hourglass wife to the score of voice-over

and steel drums—begging us to leave everything for the Panhandle, for Key West.
Always shoeless, the lovers dip; laugh at that same joke I keep wishing I could
hear through the glass. We (What? Husbands of risk; of want?) have but an hour
booked. "At least it's sunny outside." I shut the shade of the narrow window.

Now some rerun's laugh track—we must be joking. Shoeless lovers,
we dip our toes into the carpet. I shut off the lamp. I shut the blinds
like a book. "A narrow window of sunlight, but at least we'll get sunlight."
I shut my mouth; let my hand reach for his bouncing knee, his gilt finger.

The Bug

lands on my pretty man's forearm. Harmless,
it isn't deadly at all; makes his muscle flutter
—the one that gets his hand to hold mine, or
ball into a fist, or handle a gun. It's a Ladybug,
or an Asian Lady Beetle everyone mistakes
for a Ladybug—eating whatever
it lands on. My pretty man is asleep—at ease, or
plotting like the bug. Or maybe the bug
is a blowfly—eating my pretty man's tan
from his pretty arm. My man swat it
without waking, as if he's dreaming of an enemy,
or me. When my pretty man isn't asleep
he's got a temper.

                    No, he is not
asleep. He's wide awake and wants me to tell you
I'm wrong. Blowflies don't eat skin,
they lay eggs on skin. He knows all about
blowfly larvae. Napoleon used them
to clean war wounds, my cold pretty man
says in that pretty way,
with his cold pretty mouth. He's eaten plenty
of bugs before. On night watch,
over there. Over there, they're everywhere.

The Bug Chaser

Call me an eater of butterflies dancing
myself lonely. A fat dumb animal,

my mouth a mouth mouthing
all the pretty husks: God-folded

origami: easy bodies creased and unfolding
within reach of my mouth like a song

on the tip of
my tongue—that rind of sweet ruin

ruining me good. At this hour,
there are only delicious men, painted

in night, their lips flitting in and out
of trees, promising

what can not be promised.
But it's so dark here

who could make them out?
They'll live to be butterflies parading

with wings painted
in a delectable poison. Any animal hungry enough

would lap their hemlock
to sleep inside the shucked bells.

Geppetto's Lament

Off to mess with what I made him, the boy
forgets he is not a boy. Forgets these

strings and this paddle, shaped like a cross, are
in my hands. You can measure a man by

his hands. See this here thumb tip? It's the width of
a glass eye. Took my bestest knife to carve

that heartwood down to a nose then a switch.
A blade sharp enough to make a man out

of any old thing. And the tip of this finger?
Is gone. The face was tricky. He's got a

sissy's nose, a daughter's lips. Not the boy
I wished for. It was all my fault. All my

math and all my measurements were off.
And ain't even enough room in him for a heart.

Of a Wicked Boy

It dreams of a real boy's body
like the ones on the carousel braying
as each kicks the other off

his chosen horse. They're animals
threatening to buck their restraints,

trample the whimpering
organ. Of course it wants to
touch them. Why not

their skin, the splendid
bruises, the wounds, the sweet

wounds? Instead it mouths the wrong
words to their limericks as it falls
asleep beneath a tent of colluding shadows.

It dreams of their bodies taking off
by hoof in a romp. To one it begs to be

taught the game, but the boy snorts, spits
in the thing's upturned face. When it comes
to, the doll finds its wet lips

warped into a grin. At its feet,
the boy who can't stop laughing

tucks the rest of himself back
inside his pants. They're *all* laughing now.
All *touching* it—a soft hand

for every stiff limb. Their big teeth
gnash at its fingers; their knives dive

over, over. Stripped of its vest and trousers,
they go for the torso, planed crotch
in search of the city of blood and nerves

only real boys have. Pinocchio holds
still, prays to their blades, "Please, strike bone."

The Suit

A small improvised explosive device,
it went right through me, but I didn't feel
a thing. When the plucked pin missed the fabric,
how could I move? I was boot-black careful.

"Stand up straight," whispered Father as quiet
as tripwire. He ground his teeth, bone-army,
as another line was sketched where my
body should have been. "Sorry, he isn't

built right," Father told the tailor. All tots
know to stand like their dads in old war shots.
The tailor drew more hemlines, pinned new seams.
In the mirror, Father ordered me to lean

up straighter. I was a map—the lesson
of some conquered country. I'm no one's son.

"Then Practice Losing Farther; Losing Faster"

One summer, some master engineer, intent
on having the last word, hid Avalanche
Run in a building, then named the amusement

Disaster Transport. Standing at the entrance,
fingers flustered, I counted, recounted
the riders going in, but where were they spent?

Just the year before, my mother watched the descent—
each toboggan raced through the expanse
of the track faster than blood, through a bad stent,

builds a brain aneurysm. In amazement,
as if a splendid disaster, we scanned
the riders, ate paper boats of succulent

batter-dipped mushrooms, greasy beads on our chins.
But the year after, with my last parent—
my dad and his fear-wrung visor—I couldn't

quite see where the coaster or my mother went.
S'okay, dad muttered, his hand soft against
my back. In the vaster dark, a continent

full of us waited for Disaster. Cinches
once fastened in our chests, less evident
than ever before. In the outside's distant

light, I looked for my dad—my skittish master
of the shadow blood leaves behind. He gestured
in his box of light—evidently a fly.
Gulped down by darkness, I turned to Disaster.

The Black Umbrella

Left in the car, the rain caught me
without a prayer. Faith? Where
is faith's shelter when one is beaten

by rain, as if he is up to no good?
I am up to no good. A liar,
I left the umbrella

in the car. It broke. The spokes
pointed the blame
everywhere else. *The rain is revelation,*

I heard someone say once.
What did I learn? I'm still a liar. There was no umbrella
in the car, but it rained

something awful out. From inside,
I could see out the window. It was a small window—
I mean time was short.

The window was larger than I thought,
big as a car. I don't know
how long the rain stayed in my mouth

before I swallowed it. I tried to swallow,
but there was no one there. I know the window
was the size of a car because

I crashed into it. It was raining
so bad that I couldn't see. The umbrella
was black, good as new. Cell phone, I was reaching

for the cell phone. *It's bad this time*, the voice
said before the call went dead. I didn't see her,
the one with the black umbrella. She was crossing the road.

There was a body in the road—
collapsed like a broken umbrella. No, I was outside
on the ground. It was my body. The window is inside of

me. Pieces of it. I swallowed rain and blood
until help arrived. A woman
beneath a hole full of stars hovered over me.

She called my name—
or prayed? No, I couldn't see a thing.

And the Dog Comes Back

from the lake with nothing
but the bark

it left with—an unintelligible
agony. Isn't that, me

being the two-legged kind,
assumption and projection? A bark

sounds like a bark. A call of danger is a call
of ecstasy. It sloughs

the lake off its flanks,
sniffs the spittle of its chewed leash—

dangling from a hand
which too doesn't know any better.

Control yourself, the dog

is told. The impossible leash
stings its back. *So this is restraint*

—I think as the dog
feigns satisfaction

in the dull salt
of a featherless palm. No,

you've caught me. I'm not there. I'm the animal
still fucking in a stranger's bed.

His tongue licks my mouth. I whistle,
but I do not listen.

Last Night, I Was Trapped in the Wrong Body Again

A downy woodpecker shakes its head the way say a scruffy-faced
teenager might. It's pulsing—the red streak running down
the middle of its crown. Or at least I think it's red in the glow
of the bird-spiked Meijer sign. Then again, this late, I'm not sure
if it's a bird at all. It could, in fact, be a teenager. A deaf 15-year-old boy—
or he'll eventually go deaf if he doesn't turn down his earphones.
I could be anyone walking toward him.
                                Not listening to anyone,
his ears are full of wax—but even that isn't right. No one listens
to records anymore, you see. Yet his head is full of a violent song
in the same way mine could. He's dabbing at
his phone's screen like a reflection one of the Walled Lake townies might see
before they've gone too far.
                                In the winter months,
during the day, they walk on the lake
in a somnambulist's lurch. Not listening to the ice,
they pitch their huts and bore their holes in the floor. And there are fish
swishing in sequined gowns—their denticulate jaws mouthing
like background singers. All those scales
mimicking knives—a soundtrack to kill by.
                                Last night, I was trapped
in the wrong body again. I fell asleep after jacking off to a freeze frame
of Christian Bale in *American Psycho*. Then I dreamed I was Christian Bale
and couldn't stop touching myself. No, I was The Dark Knight,
only Christian Bale as The Dark Knight throwing a tantrum
on set. My cowl couldn't keep up with my pout. Then I howled myself
into myself again—big and black and terrifying. I was a monster
knocking down all of the lights. I punched someone's lights out.
                                When I came to, the woodpecker
was in my hands feeding on nothing because it was dead. Or rather, the dyed teenager
who looks like a downy woodpecker is small enough to fit in my hands.
There is no music to kill. There is nothing left to hear. The red streak is no streak
but a wound. I swear, I found him, I fished the blade out.

There Is Always a Face to Tend To

Look at your Manhunt profile: "White muscle power bottom looking

for a non-fem black top to fuck me in a mask and a hood." You want

a rape scene you saw in a movie once, a kind of beauty

only a man not used to pain prays for. "The door will be unlocked—

break in," you say. You want somebody to break you

by accident. "Harder."

                        And I am somebody

who would drive my something into yours until

we both fit the description of something else—the black boy

lurking in our imagination. Undo

the blindfold. Let's look at the son we've made—

child of our undoing. We are a double-lapped

Mary passing the blue body between us, between our two mouths

blowing then blowing some more. We are the mothers of this blue pietà.

The Lynching of Frank Embree

After the *Without Sanctuary* Photographs

1.

I've come to watch like all of the rest—
leaning-in-or-away our way through the museum.
Or watching you like the ones gathered around—pale,

gray-eyed, ghost-eyed (yes, white). They are watching me
watching you. But to watch means that you are still alive

and it's too late for that isn't it?
Object: you have become artifact: a thing I lean in or
away from. Thing, thing, thing. You are a thing. No,

your body is a sculpture made of skin, vein, and muscle.
Muscle. (So much muscle.)

If it were not for your hands, cupped together, I could see
the thing that makes you a man. Instead, a folded lozenge,
an opening to stick my mind inside of, a mouth.

2.

This is not history but pornography I've pressed
play I've come to watch your mouth move or

rather watch it beg the men (yes, white) to fill it
on camera Your mouth It's black and big It's a mouth

connected to an even blacker body *Black nigger* they say
and I reach for my body

dark and big as history Our bodies are museums
Our bodies are objects in a museum A thing a thing

3.

But you can't move in the photograph. Still life
moves in and out of you—

reflections leaning in or away. I've come to watch,
but I'm staring with an erection. My hands whisper the glass.
My thumb tip as wide as the whipper's brim. I'm grinning

as if I chased you down; tied you up
for show. My mouth spreads wide enough

4.

to swallow you I rewind and press play again To go back and watch
each man (yes, white) force you to swallow them

like a new language a new country a new gag It's funny
They mean to end you Or at least break you not like a horse

but glass in a museum encasing the past
so that I can't touch it

5.

I want to touch it, but it's too late. I've come to see
what has already happened. Looking back
like a lover being taken from behind. Falling

over my eyes, a dark hood. They mean to destroy
you. I'm afraid of your big black body,

so I too worship it when I mean to
destroy it. By "it" I'm speaking of my body too.
You with the dumb look of hope. How

dare you look at me that way?
As if I have come to save you.

6.

This is all your fault. You should have run faster.

Aaron McKinney Cleans His Magnum

With the small machine he's tender—a brush
gently works through seven small cylinders.
Then the chambers spin—not like a dervish,
but a rotary dial: no receiver,

no one to call for help. His finger in
the trigger. His baby upside down; plays
dead. From the small mouth he scrubs a stain.
As if he's wiping a man's tear away,

he dabs an oily salve across each frown
and furrow. This sad calculator is
built to subtract from and divide a town.
In another town, watching the heartless

Tin Man going on about the Wizard,
I laugh at the Scarecrow. The gun holstered.

The House

I. *Willi Ninja, Mother of the House of Ninja*

Bitch, give me a body
and I will show you how it works.

Break it down
like the math of my hands—

have you seen my hands?—
first, a blade, then a compact,

now, a mirror. What you see
is a legend on the map.

One day I will show you the world
is one big ass ball—

a house run by mothers.

II. *Transit of Venus, Daughter in the House of Xtravaganza*

I made me a sister out of this body.
I am my own mother now. There are two
of us in this one body—petite enough to fit

in any man's hands. Small
enough to run through them like our steady
rain of blond hair. We want the door-less
tower—the white body of the white girl

trapped in our mind. This body still
a tenement building towering over
nothing. They say in twenty years

you can see Venus in broad daylight
as a small speck, a mole on the face of a
big star. We've never wanted to be a

big star. Just give us a house, the picket
fence, the yellow square of butter melting
on her husband's toast. We'll be there flattening

a red and white checkered apron
like a road map across the lap.

III. *Tommye, Son Outside of the House*

Outside the house, I lift one hand
to my heart, over the inside coat pocket,

to make sure she is still there—
the little doll. But it isn't just any doll,

but my cousin's Hawaiian Fun Barbie. I am eight.
A boy. And I should know better. It's

a big house, she'll be looking for days.
I got caught once before—cross-legged

on my cousin's bedroom floor, my tongue jutting out
like a pink ribbon. When no one was looking

I braided the doll's head the way I saw
my sister braid her hair. It was my father,

my mother long gone, who yanked me up
in one heave by the arm, in the way

boys should handle dolls, in the way fathers
should not handle daughters.

Pine

And then a draft whistled dust
off the marionette, then knocked it down

where it had stood propped for months. The crash
sent gooseflesh along the boy's skin;

sent him cowering under his bed.
Up until now, the boy did all he could

to avoid touching or even glancing at the new toy
of his old body. Nights, he'd tweeze new splinters

where he missed before. Sometimes the splinters
were not splinters, but new sprigs of hair. Then

there were the nightmares: the fairy returning
to help his father fold him back

inside the coffin-body. It became clear
he didn't recognize himself,

so he'd spend hours locked in his room,
in front of the mirror, running an index finger

across the eye lashes, twisting the dark curls until
each root was close to snapping away. Now,

when he's naked, he takes inventory
of the parts; takes his father's whittling knife

to the inside of his thighs. Only the tiniest incisions
to make sure he bleeds.

Lycanthropy

As if I can't understand
my body is more than surreptitious pact

between nerve
                    and the crime it loves,

they've cornered me. And in this light
my frame is haphazard and threatening,

but I can't speak—their leather collar still cinched
around my neck, a silver

leash hook for each pair of eyes daring me
to attack. Each man armed

with a hot muzzle, a mouth
full of scripture and *no* to aim

onto my back—now bent
over a prayer they mistake

for a growl. In this place,
there is no common tongue,

I can't understand them,
so I can't follow the order

that follows each leash,
so they beat me

until skin becomes wound
then scab then hide.

& Bees

"I've sinned with my mouth and loved the sound it made."
—*Thomas Lynch*, "Attende Domine"

I listened, kept still
but the moaning
swarm came
to my ordered
field, showers
of arrows pierced
what they wanted
of the Fall's Golden
Delicious. A taste.
I only wanted a bite
of the golden bodies
at which the tiny foragers nursed.
I reached toward
the branches, eager for the weight
of all that moaning.
I didn't yield
to the boughs' swats
at my dirty hands.
I couldn't keep still,
I kept reaching,
the nectar drooled below
my wrist, pooled
in the crook of my elbow. The foragers worked
my skin, barb
by sweet barb. I bit
my lips.

I wanted

to pull back, but (Yes.)
I kept going, I took
the meat, core (Yes,
all that moaning.)
in my mouth's
mad rake, hummed,
hummed.   When I was done   I was

not done   Yes   I reached back
                inside

the branches   bent   with the sweet sweet

                                ache Overcome by the swarm

I ate the whole   sweet thing

my sweet   (Yes)   sweet body

buzzed At last   I was (Yes)

                                            a hive

The Tongue

in my mouth is as fat as a cow's tongue,
still I want to ask the woman
at the next table what she's saying
into her phone. A tongue, a cow's tongue
tastes like the rest of the cow. *Cow tastes like*

cow, an aunt once said in an accent as sweet
as Arkansas dirt. Someone, in English, told me
I don't carry my vowels like anyone
they know. I've tried, but my tongue won't move
like my aunt's nor like anyone else

in my family. I ain't makin' sense, they'd say
if they were me. Why don't I talk
like us anymore? Anyway... Every other word,
the woman slips into English. The way a train window
trades a dead city for a dead suburb;

a posh row for a cow pasture. *Duct cleaning, Thai Bistro*,
all I can make out. I happen to love the Thai Bistro,
raved about it to a friend—who's never lived
in the city or eaten Thai food. He asked,
How do you know you're not eating the tongue
of some endangered animal? I have the tongue
of some endangered animal. No one can understand me

anymore. I'm the animal on my plate
that eventually mumbles in my stomach. *Speak up!*
What are you saying?! I shout to the woman
with my inside voice. Oh well... A tongue
is a tongue is a tongue. I bet

the woman is talking about the weather;
or what she needs to pick up from the store;
or what to get __ for __'s birthday;
or __ said __ is coming to __;
or __ __ __ __.

What Are We Not For

but to be broken
like the deer resting on the side of the highway,
in a bed made of

its insides? Isn't the scene
always the same—the rump and legs
frozen in its last kick?

I too have lost my gaze,
the grip of the wheel—
like the one that plowed into

the deer. Wheel, will—it's all the same.
And the ear does fail me at times,
as it must have the deer

that should have listened better.
Francine, on the other end of the line,
tells me I'm not listening; to listen

to my body or I won't last long. We never
last long, do we? It all breaks—
the line pulsing forward, the line pause,

the long bone of it all. After all,
I am a broken animal. I am brokered
in the name of the wheel.

The Runts

It's my hand—so close

it could be bitten
clean off. Tonight

he is the dog—this bedded stranger

not using his words,
not responding to any name.

He lets me keep my hand—

returning it back cleaner
than it left. I haven't learned my lesson

so I give him the other one.

No, not *could be bitten*. He bites my hand
and I howl like something

that should not howl

down his throat. We are both dogs
now, mouthing the dark until

we are not mouthing the dark.

We are sinking in the hold
of whatever is willing to hold us.

ABOUT THE AUTHOR

image: Tarfia Faizullah

Born and raised in Detroit, TOMMYE BLOUNT now lives in
the nearby suburb of Novi, Michigan. He has been the recipient
of fellowships and scholarships from Cave Canem and Bread
Loaf Writers' Conference. His work has appeared in *Poetry*,
New England Review, *Phantom*, *Four Way Review*, *The Offing*,
Vinyl, and other publications. He holds an MFA from The MFA
Program for Writers at Warren Wilson College.